Arctic Life

Contents

Written by Sean Callery

Collins

Arctic world

The Arctic is at the far north of the Earth.

the Arctic

2

In summer it's nearly as cold as a fridge.
In winter it's three times colder than a freezer!
So how do people and animals live in the Arctic?

All year round, people wear thick coats and boots made from animal skin.

4

seal

wolverine

Seals have thick fat under their skin to keep them warm. Other animals have thick fur.

5

Houses are built on poles to keep them off the frozen ground.

Some animals make dens, which keep out
the cold wind.

People fish through holes in the ice and hunt seals.

Some animals find food under the snow.
Other animals hunt hares and seals.

Arctic hare

Arctic fox

9

Out and about

People travel on foot, by dog sled and snowmobile.

Some animals have paws, claws or flippers to help them grip the snow or swim in the sea.

Changing climate

As the Earth gets warmer, some of the ice is melting in the Arctic.

This means there's less space for people and animals to live there, and less food to eat.

In the future, people and animals may have to change the way they live.

Living in the Arctic

warm clothes

houses on stilts

14

fishing

dog sled and snowmobiles

fat and thick fur

warm dens

hunting for food

flippers to swim in the sea

Ideas for reading

Written by Clare Dowdall, PhD
Lecturer and Primary Literacy Consultant

Learning objectives: use syntax and context when reading for meaning; apply phonic knowledge and skills as the prime approach to reading unfamiliar words that are not completely decodable; read more challenging texts which can be decoded using their acquired phonic knowledge and skills, along with automatic recognition of high frequency words; identify the main events and find specific information in simple texts; distinguish fiction and non-fiction texts and the different purposes for reading them; ask and answer questions, make relevant contributions, offer suggestions and take turns

Curriculum links: Geography

High frequency words: people, who, live, about, three, than, under, their

Interest words: Arctic, contents, world, climate, north, earth, summer, winter, frozen, ice, hares, seals, snowmobile, paws, claws, melted, space, future

Resources: globe, atlas, internet, pencils, paper, whiteboard

Word count: 179

Getting started

- Show children where the Arctic circle and the Arctic are, using a globe or atlas. Ask children to share what they know about the Arctic, e.g. what animals live there; what the weather is like there. Create a *what I know* grid on the whiteboard for the Arctic to begin to establish a purpose for reading.

- Ask children what they can see on the front cover. Challenge children to raise three questions that they hope the book will answer, e.g. *what do people in the Arctic eat?*

- Turn to the back cover. Ask children to read the blurb aloud. Discuss what the blurb says and what the book intends to tell them.

- Turn to the contents page. Check children understand that this is an information book. Discuss how the contents page can be used to find information.